靈氣

Traditional Japanese Reiki Seminars

靈気療法必携

Reiki Pure and Simple

Volume II

Reiki Ryoho Hikkei
(The Most Important Methods for Reiki)

By Anny J. Slegten

Reiki Ryoho Hikkei
The Most Important Methods for Reiki)

Anny Slegten
Published by
Kimberlite Publishing House
www.kimberlitePublishingHouse.com

©2018 by Anny Slegten
All Rights Reserved. Printed in the United States.

No part of this book may be reproduced, stored in or introduced into a retrieval system, or transmitted, in any form or by any means – electronic, mechanical, photocopying, recording or otherwise – without the prior written permission of the copyright owner.

The author of this book does not dispense medical advice or prescribe the use of any technique as a form of treatment for physical, emotional, mental, spiritual or medical problems without the advice of a physician, either directly or indirectly. The intent of the author is only to offer information of a general nature to help you in your quest for physical, mental, emotional and spiritual wellbeing.

In the event you use any of the information in this book for yourself, which is your right, the author and the publisher assume no responsibility for your actions.

ISBN: 978-1-7752489-2-7
Crest design by Anny Slegten
Book cover and Kimberlite Logo designed by
Marietta Miller
www.execugraphx.com

The Kimberlite-Diamond Connection

Kimberlite is a rock type that was first categorized over a 100 years ago based on descriptions of the diamond-bearing pipes of Kimberley, South Africa.

Kimberlites are the mechanism by which diamonds are brought to the surface.

Kimberlitic rocks are the most important primary source of diamonds and the main rock type in which significant diamond deposits have been found so far.

Anny is familiar with many rocks and minerals as her husband was raised around quarries, and later worked in several mines in Canada.

Therefore, it was natural for Anny to choose kimberlite as an analogy to the soul residing within our body – as a diamond within the kimberlite.

Dedication:

With profound gratitude, I am dedicating this book to Mikao Usui who developed such a simple and effective way to make us understand the power of our focus and our intent.

In this life, having lived on three continents and observing many ethnic cultural backgrounds, the reality of life is that whoever or wherever we are, there are no "ifs" nor "buts".

The power is truly within us – that we like it or not.

With Love and Light,
Anny Slegten

Introduction

Born in Belgium in a beautiful city situated in the Flanders' Fields where the poppies grow, I was raised in a country now called La République Démocratique du Congo from 18 months old until coming to Canada at age 25. This was not a pleasant experience since I lost my country and left everything and everyone I cherished behind.

During the Independence upheaval, Immigration Officers where there, trying to entice us to move in the country they were representing.

We spoke French, and the Canadian Immigration Officer won us, explaining Canada is a bilingual country, speaking French and English – from coast to coast to coast. Well, although it is true now, it was not so at the time. When we came to Canada we quickly learned to speak English!

Experiencing life in three continents with many different nationalities, cultures, and religions, I developed a way of thinking sometimes not well understood.

English is the fifth language I learned to speak – the reason my way of explaining myself may not always feel right to you – my dear readers.

What I write has been cautiously edited to keep my identity. Should you read some of my other books, hear me in a presentation, talk to me, have a private session with me, or take one of my courses: I want to make sure you know I am the one who wrote the book.

Thank you for reading me.

With gratitude, Anny

Reiki Ryoho Hikkei

(The Most Important Methods for Reiki)

By Anny Slegten

Reiki Ryoho Hikkei Introduction
(The Most Important Methods for Reiki)

In 1999, I attended a workshop in Detroit, Michigan, USA, taught by Frank Arjava Petter, author of *Reiki Fire*, *Reiki – The Legacy of Dr Usui* and accompanied by Chetna Kobayashi – consisting of training in techniques Mikao Usui taught his students.

This was a very interesting class. There was no initiation involved during this training, only techniques, (some of them involving "table work").

Byosen; Choku Rei; Enkaku Chiryo; Gassho Meditation; Gyoshi-Ho; Heso Chiryo, and more, all the titles were written in Kanji by Chetna Kobayashi and in English by Frank Arjava Petter.

Very self conscious of her handwriting, we were asked to honour Chetna's request to not photocopy the Kanji and make our own. Back to Sherwood Park, Alberta, Canada I was introduced to a Japanese Scholar fluent in the Japanese language who reads and writes the old and new Kanji, Hiragana and Katakana.

These meetings were a course by themselves on Japanese traditions and what we Westerners call "symbols".

It was a pleasure and a privilege to attend this class, which is one of the reasons I have decided to share the information with you.

I hope you are enjoying this information as much as I did.

Love and Light,

Anny Slegten

Table of Contents

Dedication	VII
Anny's Introduction	IX
Reiki Ryoho Hikkei Introduction (The Most Important Methods for Reiki)	XIII
Gassho Meditation *(Two Hands coming together)*	*17*
Kenyoku *(Dry bathing)*	*21*
Joshin Kokyu Ho *(Breathing exercise to purify the mind)*	*27*
Reiki Undo *(Reiki exercise devised by Mrs Koyama)*	*33*
Heso Chiryo *(Navel healing technique for relaxation)*	*41*
Reiji Technique *(Directed by a god)* **(Table work)**	*45*
Koki- Ho *(Healing with the breath)*	*51*
Gyoshi -Ho and Yoki-Ho *(Healing with the eyes)*	*55*
Byosen *(scanning)*	*61*
Jacki Kiri Joka Ho *(Cutting off negative energy)*	*67*
Sei heki chiryo *(Healing bad habits)*	*73*
Reiki Mawashi *(Reiki current)*	*77*
Shu Chu Reiki *(Concentrated Reiki)* **(Table work)**	*81*

Enkaku Chiryo *(Distant Healing)*	87
Shashin Chiryo *(Photo Healing)*	87
Fox Technique or Kanguru Technique **(Table work)**	97
Reiki Undo with a Group	103
Second Degree Usui Reiki Symbols	111
Choku Rei - The Power Symbol	117
Sei Heki - The Mental Healing Symbol	125
Hon Sha Ze Sho Nen - The Distant Healing Symbol	131
Mikao Usui, Reiki and the Japanese Culture -	137
Mrs. Hawayo Takata	165
Online Store, Contact and More	173
Other Books By Anny Slegten	175
Who is Anny Slegten?	181

Blank pages after each exercise are supplied to allow you to journal your experience..

The Gassho Meditation
Hands clasped in praying position

Workshop Hand-out

The Japanese word Gassho means two hands (are) coming together. Practice this meditation either sitting on the floor or on a chair in the morning or the evening for twenty to thirty minutes.

Close your eyes and relax. Fold your hands in front of your heart in a relaxed way in the Gassho position. Concentrate your total attention on the point where both middle fingers meet and forget the world around you. If sitting in this fashion should become uncomfortable, let your hands gently and slowly come down and rest on your lap. Let them still be folded and keep your attention on the required point.

Anny Slegten's notes:
- *Spine erected.*
- *Hands in prayer position.*
- *Focus on the middle fingers touching.*
- *Tongue touching the upper palate.*
- *Spine straight and erect.*

Breathe in through the nose, breathe out through the mouth, and listen to your body: Pay attention to the physical sensations, a tickling, a pain, whatever: your body is « talking » to you.

Do this for twenty minutes. At the end, let your hands drop gently and slowly on your lap, enjoy the inner quietness, and come back to this room.

The Gassho Meditation
Hands clasped in praying position

Your impressions and insights:

The Gassho Meditation
Hands clasped in praying position

Your impressions and insights:

Kenyoku

«Dry bathing», cleansing.

Workshop Hand-Out

The Kenyoku technique – Dry Bathing.

Kenyoku is a Japanese word that literally means dry bathing. It is a technique to strengthen your energy and disconnect yourself from people, things, situations, even your own thoughts and emotions.

Put your right hand on the left side of your chest, over the collar bone. Now stroke down gently across your chest to the right hip bone. Do the same with your left hand, starting on the right side of your chest, above the collar bone. Stroke down gently towards your left hip bone.

Repeat the movement with your right hand.

Now put your right hand on your left shoulder and stroke down gently over your arm and the palm of your hand, down past your finger tips. Do the same stroke with your left hand over your right arm and repeat the pattern once more with your right hand stroking along your left arm.

(This technique was taught to Frank Arjava Petter by someone who used to be a Buddhist monk. In the former Buddhist monk school of Reiki they add a Gassho at the end of the Kenyoku technique).

乾浴

Kenyoku
«Dry bathing», cleansing.

<u>*Your impressions and insights:*</u>

Kenyoku

«Dry bathing», cleansing.

<u>Anny Slegten's notes</u> :

Ken = Dry
Yoku = Bathing

To clean the slate. Right hand on left shoulder down to right hip bone. Left hand on right shoulder down to left hip bone. Right hand on left shoulder down to right hip bone.

<u>Then</u> (Usui method) Right hand from over left palm from wrist to finger tips. Left hand from over right palm from wrist to finger tips. Right hand from over left palm from wrist to finger tips.

<u>Or</u>
Inside of arm
<u>Or</u>
Outside of arm

<u>Note: 3 times each</u>!

To be done with the intent of clearing before and after giving a session.

This is very much like the « Energy Sweep » practiced by Toshikata Mochizuki's Reiki students.

It is interesting to note that in Japan, the number 4 is bad luck just as 13 is regarded as bad luck in the western world. Buildings in Japan do not have a 4th floor just like we do not have a 13th floor here!

Kenyoku
«Dry bathing», cleansing.

Your impressions and insights:

Kenyoku
«Dry bathing», cleansing.

<u>*Your impressions and insights:*</u>

Joshin Kokyu-Ho

Breathing exercise to purify the mind.

Workshop Hand-Out

The Japanese phrase Joshin Kokyu-Ho means breathing exercise to purify the spirit. This is a breathing technique to strengthen your energy, collect energy in your tanden* and learn to let the energy flow through your hands.

Breathe in through your nose and imagine drawing Reiki energy into your body through the crown chakra. Draw the energy down to your tanden*. When the breath has reached your tanden*, keep it there for a few seconds without straining and imagine it to be permeating your whole body.

Then breathe out through your mouth and imagine that the energy flows out through your finger tips, your hand chakras, the tips of your toes and the foot chakras.

Anny Slegten's notes :

*To locate the tanden, pay attention to you lower abdomen. Stand relaxed, feet apart just under your shoulders – and slowly bend your knees until you feel like a rock just under the belly button.

To feel the energy: Breathe in through your nose and crown chakra into the tanden. Feel the energy expand in the tanden.

Then, breathe the energy out through the palms of your hands, your finger tips, the soles of your feet and the tips of your toes.

Joshin Kokyu-Ho

Breathing exercise to purify the mind.

Your impressions and insights:

Joshin Kokyu-Ho

Breathing exercise to purify the mind.

Note:

Mikao Usui instructed that the energy flows through the palms of our hands as well as through our fingertips.

When administering Reiki, he was using the palms of his hands as well as his finger tips, much like in Qi Gong.

Putting your tongue on the roof of your mouth is not in Mikao Usui's instructions.

Joshin Kokyu-Ho

Breathing exercise to purify the mind.

<u>*Your impressions and insights:*</u>

浄心呼吸法

Joshin Kokyu-Ho
Breathing exercise to purify the mind.

<u>*Your impressions and insights:*</u>

浄心呼吸法

Reiki Undo

Reiki (energy) exercise

Workshop Hand-Out

The breathing technique Reiki Undo was devised by Mrs Koyama, the sixth president of the Usui Reiki Ryoho Gakkai. The Japanese word Undo means exercise.

Sit or stand in the Gassho position and pray for the Reiki energy to come through you. Say to yourself: Reiki Undo begin. If you are practicing with a partner, touch his/her shoulders from behind and allow your body to move, whichever way it wants to move. Breathe in deeply and let go as much as you can when you are breathing out. After a few deep breaths your body will probably start to move.

If the movement doesn't come through you easily, be patient and don't create anything. Keep doing this exercise for at least three months on a daily basis.

Anny Slegten's notes :

This is an exercise to be done once a day. Energy radiates from our entire body. This is an exercise to let the energy move our body so it can self-regulate itself.

Take a few deep breaths and let the body move.

It can take some time before the body starts to move, therefore simply « jump start » the process.

Reiki Undo

Reiki (energy) exercise

<u>*Your impressions and insights:*</u>

霊気運動

Reiki Undo
Reiki (energy) exercise

In the beginning, you will have to « jump start » several times before getting into the mode.

<u>*To jump start:*</u>
1. *Thumbs in, arms extended forward, breathe in.*
2. *Breathe out as you <u>tense</u> your body, bring the elbows back to your body and totally let go as you go into the « mode ».*

By letting the energy move the body, the energy moves the blocks and the body starts to discharge the toxins and functions properly.

<u>*When alone*</u>*, follow your body needs 10 to 40 minutes.*

<u>*In a group*</u>*, the energy usually slows down after 10 minutes.*

When « coming back », quietly look at the body from the inside.

There is a similar technique in Indonesia called «TOUYOU».

<u>*Note :*</u>
When I observed the demonstration I found it looked very much like when Ramtha enters JZ Knight's body and aligns his energy to the body he just entered

Reiki Undo

Reiki (energy) exercise

Your impressions and insights:

霊気運動

Reiki Undo

Reiki (energy) exercise

<u>Reiki (energy) exercise</u>

A student sitting in a chair suddenly started to move in an erratic way during a Reiki Undo practice. I observed her - making sure she was safe.

At the end of it all, she opened her eyes in total surprise, feeling very comfortable in her body.

During the exercise, observing how her body was moving, she realised it was re-doing all the movements she had made while attempting to break a fall from her bicycle a few days earlier.

Having allowed her body to move freely resulted in her body being back in alignment, feeling great and comfortable from the top of her head to tips of her toes.

Reiki Undo

Reiki (energy) exercise

<u>*Your impressions and insights:*</u>

霊気運動

Reiki Undo

Reiki (energy) exercise

Your impressions and insights:

霊気運動

Heso Chiryo
Navel treatment

Workshop Hand-Outs

The Japanese word Heso means navel and the word Chiryo means treatment. Put your middle finger into your navel and apply a little pressure until you feel your pulse. Let the Reiki energy flow into your navel until you feel that your pulse and the energy are in harmony.

Practice for 5-10 minutes.

Anny Slegten's notes
Frank Arjava Petter learned this method at the end of August 1999, about 10 days before giving the workshop.

Put your middle finger in your navel.

The energy will flow into your navel and do it until the pulse of the finger is in harmony with the energy of the navel. Breathe the energy into your body. This technique is practiced in several energy methods.

It is supposed to relax the body to be calm, collected and centered.

Note :
While in the womb, we are connected to our life source by the umbilical cord (the navel). I learned in a workshop in Kinesiology that the navel is one of the most important parts of our body.

This method restores the connection into the life force, healing the feeling of being alone.

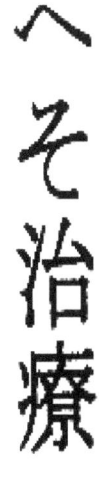

Kanji

Hiragana / Kanji

Heso Chiryo
Navel treatment

<u>*Your impressions and insights:*</u>

Kanji

Hiragana / Kanji

Heso Chiryo
Navel treatment

<u>*Your impressions and insights:*</u>

臍治療

Kanji

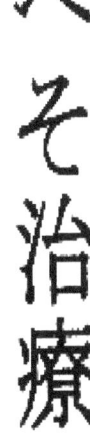

Hiragana / Kanji

The Reiji Technique
Directed (or shown) by a god or higher person.

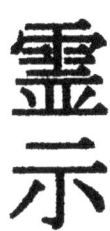

Workshop Hand-Out

Reiji is a Japanese word that literally means indication of the spirit/energy.

It describes a short but potent prayer that is repeated within the heart of the practitioner before giving treatments. It makes us aware of the fact that we are mere channels for the universal life energy and teaches us to learn to listen to our intuition.

Reiji has three parts:

1- Fold your hands in the Gassho position. Pray to the Reiki energy to flow through you.
2- Pray for the healing and well being of your client on all levels.
3- Move your folded hands in front of your third eye. Ask the Reiki energy to guide your hands to where they are needed.

Now proceed with the healing. Follow your hands and be aware of any changes in the body as you touch it. Be aware of your own thoughts/emotions and your intuition.

Anny Slegten's notes : *(« Table work »)*
The Reiji technique is a powerful prayer and is to be used prior to starting a treatment. It teaches our energy to flow by intuition.

The Reiji Technique
Directed (or shown) by a god or higher person.

Your impressions and insights:

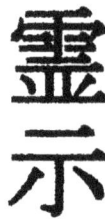

The Reiji Technique

Directed (or shown) by a god or higher person.

<u>*To increase our intuition* –</u>

1. *Put your hands in prayer at heart level until you feel hooked up.*
2. *Pray for the healing of the client.*
3. *Raise the hands to your third eye and ask the energy in your hands to guide your hands to where it is needed.*

<u>THEN</u>

4. put your hands **<u>GENTLY</u>** on the client's crown chakra and wait until there is an impulse or inspiration, and follow your hands.

<u>Your hands will lift up when no longer needed.</u>

- *Mikao Usui was tapping with his fingertips or touching with the palm of his hands. He would touch, rub, massage, or tap* **<u>GENTLY</u>**.

- *Mikao Usui was also mimicking the client to find out what the body language was saying.*

- *Mikao Usui said the hand positions are like a crutch until you do it by intuition*

The Reiji Technique
Directed (or shown) by a god or higher person.

Your impressions and insights:

The Reiji Technique
Directed (or shown) by a god or higher person.

<u>*Your notes impressions and insights:*</u>

靈
氣

Koki-Ho

Healing with the breath:

<u>Workshop Hand-Out</u>

The Japanese word Koki means breath or breathing, healing with the breath. Not only do we breathe energy in, we also breathe it out!

Draw a symbol, mainly the Power Symbol with your tongue on the roof of your mouth while breathing in.

Breathe out and blow at the diseased/injured body part, imagining that the symbol is projected onto it.

It helps to visualize the symbol blown onto the particular body part.

<u>Anny Slegten's notes</u> :

In an interview, Mikao Usui said "It (Reiki Healing Techniques) uses only looking, blowing, stroking, light tapping and touching".

Basically, it is blowing on the burn, pain, wound with the intention of blowing it away. Very much like what mothers do.

1. *Breathe in through your nose and draw the energy down to your tanden.*
2. *Draw a symbol, mainly the Power Symbol with your tongue on the roof of your mouth while breathing in.*
3. *Blow out Reiki on the burn, pain, wound with the intention of blowing it away.*

You can also do this on a photo in Distant Healing.

Koki-Ho

Healing with the breath:

<u>*Your impressions and insights:*</u>

呼気法

Koki-Ho

Healing with the breath:

Your impressions and insights:

呼気法

靈
氣

Gyoshi-Ho
Healing with the eyes

Workshop Hand-Out

The Japanese word Gyoshi means staring. In his handbook Dr. Usui says that energy radiates from all the body parts, mostly from the hands, the eyes and the breath of the Initiate.

We are used to throwing our energy out through our eyes, but with this technique we learn to use it. In order to heal we must first defocus our eyes.

Staring is aggressive and an aggressive look does not heal – it intrudes. With soft focus look at the body part you want to treat for a few minutes. While you are looking at the other, try to let the image of the other enter your eyes instead of actively looking. Notice how a circle of energy between you and the other is created when you let the energy of the other enter your eyes. Project the symbols to the body part you want to treat.

Anny Slegten's notes :

We waste a lot of energy with our eyes. This technique teaches us to use that energy instead.

Yoki Ho is a look that can convey happiness or give you a creepy feeling, depending how it is written.

Practice :
1- *When we stare and hurt the other person. We started first with an exercise before this exercise: For 2 minutes, we were to look in our partner's eyes with a judgemental stare.*

YOKI
Happy/Kind
Stare

YOKI
Ghostly/Creepy
Stare

Gyoshi-Ho
Healing with the eyes

Your impressions and insights:

凝視法

陽気

YOKI
Happy/Kind
Stare

妖気

YOKI
Ghostly/Creepy
Stare

Gyoshi-Ho
Healing with the eyes

> 2- *Now, de-focus and see your partner as perfect. In a constructive way, de-focus your eyes. It creates a circle between object or person and you. You let the person or object come to you.*

<u>Note</u> : *As I was doing this practice, all of a sudden I saw my partner's 2 eyes plus the Third Eye.*

De-focus your eyes on the person's body part that you want to heal. Remember to project an appropriate symbol to stay focussed on the intent.

凝視法

陽気

YOKI
Happy/Kind
Stare

妖気

YOKI
Ghostly/Creepy
Stare

Gyoshi-Ho
Healing with the eyes

<u>*Your impressions and insights:*</u>

凝視法

陽気

YOKI
Happy/Kind Stare

妖気

YOKI
Ghostly/Creepy Stare

Gyoshi-Ho

Healing with the eyes

<u>*Your impressions and insights:*</u>

凝視法

陽気

YOKI
Happy/Kind Stare

妖気

YOKI
Ghostly/Creepy Stare

Byosen
Scanning

Worshop Hand-Out

The Japanese word Byosen means sick (diseased) line.

Fold your hands in the Gassho position in front of your heart. Pray that the energy will come through you and guide you to the part that needs treatment. If your hands are pulled to a body part immediately – follow it.

If not, place your dominant hand above the crown chakra of the client and tune in. If this doesn't work scan the body, front and back, in slow downward movements.

You may feel a tingling sensation in your hands. It may be a feeling of heat or just a deep knowing that you have found the right spot.

Be aware.

When you touch the body part, this feeling can become quite uncomfortable and move up your arm, into the shoulder. Stay with it and wait for the sensation to trace back down your arm, and out of your hands, then move to the next position.

病泉

Byosen
Scanning

Your impressions and insights:

Byosen
Scanning

Anny Slegten's notes :

With this method you learn to find and treat negatively charged body parts.

Direct positive energy into the negative energy of the subject.

While scanning, you feel it.

If the client's pain moves up your arm, hold the position until the client's pain withdraws from your arm and hand.

When you are good at this, you just connect and let the positive energy follow your hand.

Directions

1- The Gassho meditation
2- The Kenyoku (Dry Bathing or Energy Brush down)
3- Then let the energy flow and do the scanning.

Note : this is a <u>kinetic reading</u>.

Byosen
Scanning

病泉

<u>*Your impressions and insights:*</u>

Byosen
Scanning

<u>*Your impressions and insights:*</u>

病泉

Jacki Kiri Joka Ho

A method to cut off, cleanse bad energy.

Workshop Hand-Out

The Japanese word Jacki means negative and the word Kiri (from the verb Kiru) means to cut. Cut off negative energy from any object by horizontally cutting through the air with your dominant hand about 2 inches (5 centimetres) above the object three times. After the third time stop the movement abruptly.

While practicing stay centered in your tanden and hold your breath.

Do not, under any circumstances use this technique on humans or other sentient beings!

Anny Slegten's notes :

Bad energy	cutting	cleansing	method
Jacki	Kiri	Joka	Ho

For removing, cleansing, clearing an energy of a bad situation or an object.
- *Hold the object in one hand, or if too heavy have it on a table or hold it in your imagination.*
- *Breathe in,*
- *Hold your breath as you cut the energy with the other hand.*
Slash movement -- 1
                -- 2
                -- 3 stop abruptly just above it.

- *Breathe out.*

Once you have neutralized it – remove the energy and energize as you wish.

Jacki Kiri Joka Ho
A method to cut off, cleanse bad energy.

<u>*Your impressions and insights:*</u>

邪気切り 浄化法

Jacki Kiri Joka Ho

A method to cut off, cleanse bad energy.

Note :

Mikao Usui used to energize crystal balls for people to put on themselves while he was away.

Remember it is important to cleanse a crystal/object and re-energize it before using it again since the crystal/object has taken on the undesirable energy and could be passed on to someone else.

邪気切り　浄化法

Jacki Kiri Joka Ho
A method to cut off, cleanse bad energy.

<u>*Your impressions and insights:*</u>

邪気切り　浄化法

Jacki Kiri Joka Ho
A method to cut off, cleanse bad energy.

<u>*Your impressions and insights:*</u>

邪気切り　浄化法

Sei Heki Chiryo
Healing bad habits

Workshop Hand-Out

In this case the Japanese word Sei Heki is translated as healing or removing cravings and bad habits.

Create an affirmation that is short and to the point.

Place your dominant hand on the back of the head of the receiver (or yourself) and your non dominant hand on the forehead. Say the affirmation in your mind for a couple of minutes.

Now take away the non-dominant hand from the forehead and give Reiki to the back of the head for a few minutes-as long as it feels right.

Anny Slegten's notes :

This was demonstrated to us:

Frank Arjava Petter asked for a volunteer. It turned out the lady wanted to quit smoking. It took a while to formulate an affirmation on the beneficial reasons to quit. In this case, it was « because I care about myself »

The affirmation flows as you hold the head in the Emotional Stress Release Mode for a few minutes.

Let go of the forehead and hold and Reiki the back of the head for about 5 minutes.

Then let go of it all.

Sei Heki Chiryo
Healing bad habits

<u>*Your impressions and insights:*</u>

性癖治療

Sei Heki Chiryo
Healing bad habits

Your impressions and insights:

性癖治療

靈
氣

Reiki Mawashi

Moving current from one place to the other.

Workshop Hand-Out

The Japanese word Mawashi means current. In this exercise a current of Reiki energy is passed through a group of practitioners.

Sit in a circle and hold hands, or hold your hands a few inches above/below the hands of your neighbours. Your left hand facing up, the right one facing down.

The teacher starts the energy flow, sending energy to his/her left. The receiver receives the energy from his/her right hand, lets it flow through his/her body and passes it on to the next person through his/her left hand. Practice for 10 minutes.

Try it the other way around as well.

Anny Slegten's notes:

This is the « energy balancing » I make my students do prior to group « tablework ».

The group is arranged around the table – holding hands. This includes the hands of the person who will receive Reiki on the table.

The left hands of everyone are facing up, and the right hands are facing down. I make them breathe the energy in through their left hand facing up, and breathe out through their right hand facing down.

Reiki Mawashi
Moving current from one place to the other.

Your impressions and insights:

Reiki Mawashi

Moving current from one place to the other.

<u>*Your impressions and insights:*</u>

Shu Chu Reiki

Concentrated or done in a group.

The Japanese word Shu Chu literally means concentrated. This technique is practiced in a group or at a Reiki meeting.

Each group member gives energy to one group member wishing and praying for their happiness and health. First degree Reiki Practitioners lay their hands upon the client and second degree Reiki Practitioners may use the Reiki symbols.

Second degree practitioners can do this via distant healing as well.

This can be an intense experience for the client. Because of this, Frank Arjava Petter would not recommend treating clients who are emotionally unstable with many practitioners.

<u>**Anny Slegten's notes:**</u>*«Table work»*

We were instructed to first cleanse ourselves with the Kenyoku technique (dry bathing) and then do the Reiji technique:
- *1- Pray*
- *2- Up the brow chakra to let the energy guide your hands.*
- *3- Put your hands where they want to go.*

Shu Chu Reiki is what Toshikata Moshisuki calls «Marathon Reiki».

Since Frank Arjava Petter did not instruct the participants to first balance their energy prior to administering Reiki, I decided to « learn by observing » and watched the group instead of participating in this exercise.

Shu Chu Reiki
Concentrated or done in a group.

<u>*Your impressions and insights:*</u>

Shu Chu Reiki
Concentrated or done in a group.

After the practice, back to our chairs, the lady who was sitting next to me wondered how come I did not participate in this exercise and reported feeling sick during that session.

Note:

To end the 2 minute practices (everyone at each table was taking turns), Frank Arjava Petter touched the round hand music cymbals together, but did it in a way where there was <u>NO SOUND</u>. His intention was signaling an end to the exercise – and the class responded.

Shu Chu Reiki
Concentrated or done in a group.

<u>*Your impressions and insights:*</u>

Shu Chu Reiki
Concentrated or done in a group.

Your impressions and insights:

Enkaku Chiryo
Sending Treatment (Distant Healing).

Workshop Hand-Out

Enkaku Chiryo, Distant Healing. There are as many distant healing techniques as there are Reiki practitioners. This technique is Dr. Usui's version of it.

The Japanese word Enkaku means sending and the word Chiryo means treatment. This method has also been known in Japan as Shashin Chiryo:

Shashin Chiryo or photographic treatment:

Treatment using a picture, a photograph. There must be as many distant healing methods as there are Reiki practitioners all of which are designed to help focus our minds.

If possible use a photograph of the recipient. Write her/his name and date of birth on the back. If you have been asked to send energy on behalf of someone you don't personally know, try to gather additional information and write that on the photograph as well. This helps you to focus your energy. If you don't have a picture of the recipient, draw an idol representing the other person on one of your fingers, or on your knee, and use that instead. Frank Arjava Petter suggested not to send energy to a person who has not asked you specifically for it.

SHASHIN CHIRYO

Photographic Treatment

Enkaku Chiryo
Sending Treatment (Distant Healing).

<u>*Your impressions and insights:*</u>

遠隔治療

写真治療

SHASHIN CHIRYO

Photographic Treatment

Enkaku Chiryo

Sending Treatment (Distant Healing).

<u>Anny Slegten's notes</u> :

It is helpful to have a photograph. On the back of the photo – write name, date of birth, plus as much information as possible about that person: Profession, etc., including who that person is related to in the group.

When Mikao Usui did not have a picture, even if he knew what the person looked like, he would draw the sick person either on his knee or on one of his fingers and focus the healing on it.

Personally, I am against this practice. I learned the method of using the upper legs to represent the person to whom the healing is to be sent when attending more than ten Reiki classes from different Reiki Masters/Teachers.

When one draws the sick person on one's body, we in fact draw the sickness on us. The problem is disengaging once the healing is completed.

Therefore, I recommend the use of a Teddy Bear, any stuffed animal, or even a doll. It helps with « following our hands » and with disconnecting from the person at the end of the session.

Although the Reiki Energy is going trough time and space, removing watches and rings before a Reiki session, or making "an appointment » with the person who will have the distant healing is totally at the practitioner's discretion. It is important to follow one's belief system.

SHASHIN CHIRYO

Photographic Treatment

Enkaku Chiryo
Sending Treatment (Distant Healing).

<u>*Your impressions and insights:*</u>

遠隔治療

写真治療

SHASHIN CHIRYO

Photographic Treatment

Enkaku Chiryo

Sending Treatment (Distant Healing).

There are also many questions about asking permission to send Reiki.

You will know when the Reiki is refused by getting it back in your face, even if permission was granted.

When I learned Reiki, the Reiki Master/Teacher explained to us she was regularly sending Reiki to a very sick member of her family, to get it back in her face.

The member of the family was very angry at her, having being confronted with a very sensitive situation. She kept sending him Reiki energy, and did this for a long time.

And then, the magic happened: the Reiki started to be accepted, and a much needed reconciliation happened.

Personally, I do not ask permission to send Reiki. To my understanding, it is usually the soul who is calling for help.

Therefore, having bypassed the critical brain, it is the soul who will either accept or reject the help offered.

When doing a group distant healing on <u>one</u> subject, I am asking the practitioners to balance their energy first.

SHASHIN CHIRYO

Photographic Treatment

Enkaku Chiryo
Sending Treatment (Distant Healing).

Your impressions and insights:

遠隔治療

写真治療

SHASHIN CHIRYO

Photographic Treatment

Enkaku Chiryo
Sending Treatment (Distant Healing)..

Some people need hard proof of everything. Although a true story, the name of the Reiki Master/Teacher practitioner friend of mine has been changed to protect her identity as well as the identity of her husband who she invited to come along.

Betty is a Reiki Master/Teacher practitioner friend of mine.

Betty had arranged a Reiki Circle where participants take turns laying on the table while receiving Reiki from other participants.

Betty's husband was very skeptical about the validity of it all. He was especially sceptical of "Distant Healing" and was saying very derogatory comments as he watched the women taking turns on the table.

Once all the women had enjoyed a Reiki session, they consulted each other while Betty's husband was not paying attention. Then Betty invited him to lie down on the table to participate. As he laid on his back, he again made fun of all these ladies practicing Reiki.

These women were on top of things and knew what to do. Standing about one metre from the table so there was no physical contact – the practitioners started to do "Distant Healing" by beaming Reiki on his "Private Parts." Suddenly, Betty's husband experienced an erection he could not believe! So powerful, so visible, he turned over on the table in an attempt to hide it... Completely embarrassed!

He certainly learned the hard way.

SHASHIN CHIRYO

Photographic Treatment

Enkaku Chiryo
Sending Treatment (Distant Healing).

<u>*Your impressions and insights:*</u>

遠隔治療

写真治療

SHASHIN CHIRYO

Photographic Treatment

Enkaku Chiryo
Sending Treatment (Distant Healing).

<u>*Your impressions and insights:*</u>

遠隔治療

写真治療

SHASHIN CHIRYO

Photographic Treatment

Fox Technique or Kangaroo Technique
The Laser Fox. The Laser Hoe.

No Workshop Hand-outs given

<u>Anny Slegten's notes</u> (« Table work »)
There is some similarity with the « Tripod » technique learned from Reiki Master/Teacher Trish Dennison and the « Ultrasound » technique in Healing Touch. This is also taught by a branch of the Reiki Alliance.

<u>Left hand</u>: All fingers touching the left thumb.

<u>Right hand</u>: The two central fingers touching the right thumb.

We were instructed to work on a partner laying on a table – look at that person while holding the left hand turned up, and all fingers touching the left thumb – with the intent of connecting and receiving Universal Energy. Close our eyes and imagine we have X-Ray vision of the person and let the laser (right hand) just hoover above the person where the energy guides us.

Please understand we all have our personal way to experience the « X-Ray vision ». For me, I see thick black lines on the body where my « laser » is directed.

During this exercise, I saw a thick black line along the bottom of the rib cage. My hand got stuck above Margo's navel and a sharp pain made my hand jump. I then gently drew « it » out, and that was it.

きつねテクニック

Fox Technique

カンガルーテクニック

Kangaroo Technique

Fox Technique or Kangaroo Technique
The Laser Fox. The Laser Hoe.

<u>*Your impressions and insights:*</u>

きつねテクニック

Fox Technique

カンガルーテクニック

Kangaroo Technique

Fox Technique or Kangaroo Technique

The Laser Fox. The Laser Hoe.

Standing there, eyes closed, the X-Ray vision went blank. I opened my eyes, looked at Margo and put both hands on her lower arm.

Later, Margo explained her stomach burped and the discomfort vanished (an indigestion from too much coffee at breakfast that morning). Margo also thanked me for putting both hands or her arm!

Nobody had touched her that way since she left home to take several courses three weeks prior to this one and it comforted her to be touched on the arm.

きつねテクニック
Fox Technique

カンガルーテクニック
Kangaroo Technique

Fox Technique or Kangaroo Technique
The Laser Fox. The Laser Hoe.

<u>*Your impressions and insights:*</u>

きつねテクニック

Fox Technique

カンガルーテクニック

Kangaroo Technique

Fox Technique or Kangaroo Technique
The Laser Fox. The Laser Hoe.

<u>*Your impressions and insights:*</u>

きつねテクニック
Fox Technique

カンガルーテクニック
Kangaroo Technique

Reiki Undo with a Group

Reiki (energy) exercise with a group

Workshop Hand-Out

Create a train of several people – one sitting on the knees behind the other. Each one is lightly touching the shoulders of the person in front.

Start by saying to yourselves – Reiki Undo start and follow the energy. Don't do anything, let it happen.

For this exercise you need some space and you must make sure that tables and things that could physically hurt the participants are moved away. It should be done in a place that allows for a relatively high noise level!

This exercise creates a lot of energy and instantaneous healing may occur.

Anny Slegten's notes :

I was not there when this was practised. I could hear the laughter from where I was waiting for the taxi to drive me back to the airport where I was catching the last plane to my destination.

The Reiki train is a wonderful and truly enjoyable way to release the stress of leaving a group.

The one at the front of the "train" has the privilege of receiving Reiki from the one at the end of the "train".

Regarding the Reiki train exercises, I will share with you some very interesting energy demonstrations that I learned in Touch for Health classes.

Reiki Undo with a Group
Reiki (energy) exercise with a group.

<u>*Your impressions and insights:*</u>

霊気運動

Reiki Undo with a Group

Reiki (energy) exercise with a group.

For whatever reason – when working on a person that is not co-operating – I learned a method in kinesiology (a muscle testing procedure) to "put on" the energy of the person the practitioner wants to work on.

There are many reasons for someone not to co-operate – including feeling nothing when kinetic corrections are needed.

We were told to sit in a semi-circle, with the "The Subject" – the person who needed the corrections placed at the front.

The person at the back of the semi-circle "The Surrogate" is removed from the semi-circle and then "puts on" the energy of "The Subject" needing corrections.

Yvette Eastman, our teacher and Kinesiologist Guru then made all the needed corrections on The Surrogate.

Once the corrections were completed, "The Surrogate" returns to the back of the semi-circle.

The Kinesiologist then asked everyone in the semi-circle to touch the shoulder of the person next to them in order to connect The Subject and The Surrogate energetically

Once the connection was made through us all, we were asked to let go.

Reiki Undo with a Group

Reiki (energy) exercise with a group.

<u>*Your impressions and insights:*</u>

Reiki Undo with a Group

Reiki (energy) exercise with a group.

The muscle testing clearly showed The Subject benefited from the correction.

Explaining this during an advanced hypnotherapy class, a student busted into laughter.

Her father, who is a farmer, was walking along his farm's electric fence. He was holding hands with his date, a city dweller.

At one point, he asked her, "Here, give me a kiss" and touched the electric fence as they kissed. He felt nothing since he was the conduit. She did...!

It had been years since her father married the city dweller - and her mother still remembers "The Kiss."

Reiki Undo with a Group

Reiki (energy) exercise with a group.

Your impressions and insights:

Reiki Undo with a Group

Reiki (energy) exercise with a group.

<u>*Your impressions and insights:*</u>

Usui Reiki written affirmations we call "Symbols"

Workshop Hand-Out :

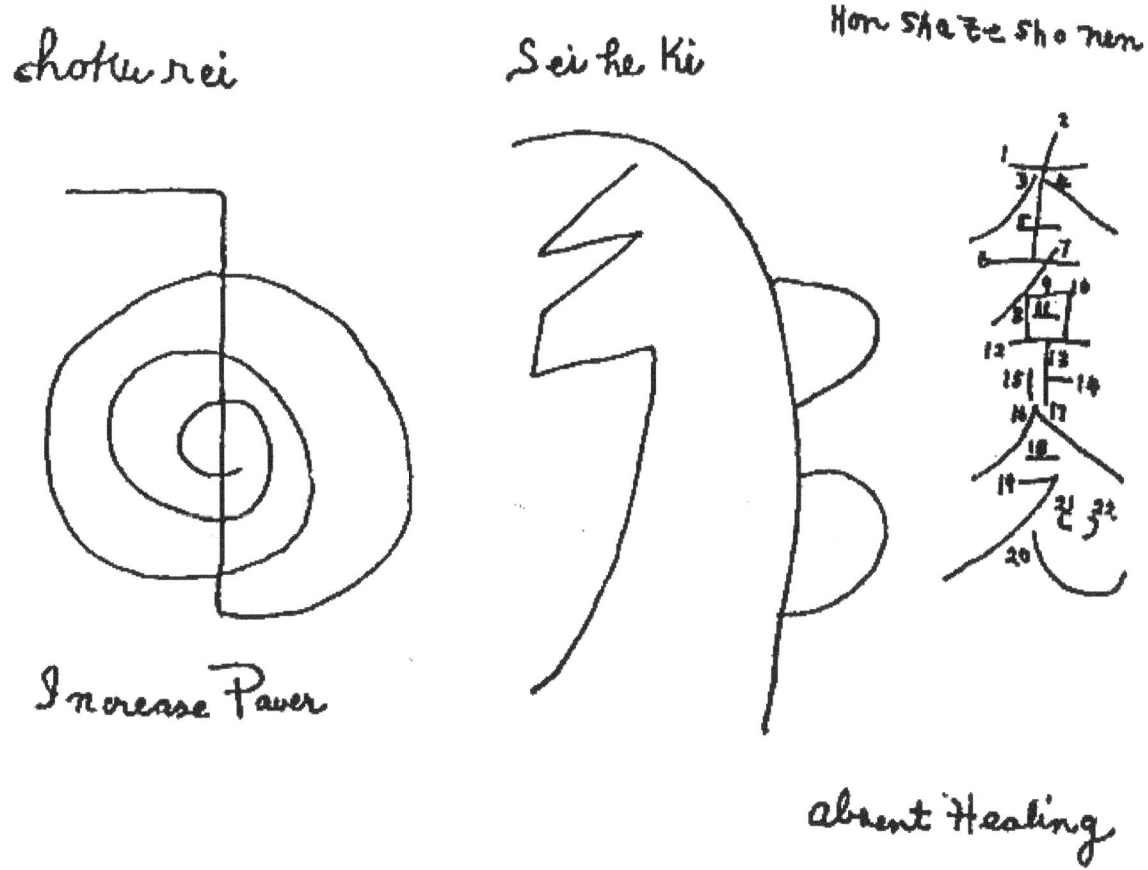

This hand-out is the same as the one I received from William Rand in February 1995.

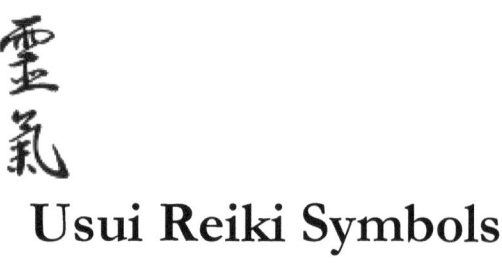

Usui Reiki Symbols

Your impressions and insights:

Usui Reiki Symbols

The Usui Reiki system uses four « symbols ». What we Westerners call « symbols » are in fact written statements or affirmations. Mikao Usui used a writing understood by educated people of the time. I often ponder had Mikao Usui lived in Europe – would he have written all these affirmations in Latin.

In the pages that follow, I am sharing with you:

- *What I learned at the Japanese Reiki Techniques workshop.*
- *What I have learned from other Reiki Master/Teachers.*
- *Once back in Canada – what I learned when meeting a Japanese Scholar after the course given by Frank Arjava Petter in Detroit, Michigan, U.S.A.*
- *What I found out through my research for the original intent of the Usui Reiki System and my understanding of it all.*

Please note: Japanese people are very self conscious on how they write – the reason Frank Arjava Petter asked us to honour Chetna's request to draw the Japanese writing ourselves or find some one who will do it for us.

All the printed and hand brushed Japanese writing in this book was given to me by the Japanese Scholar I met in Edmonton, Alberta, Canada. Having not done it by hand for some time, and after some hesitation, the Japanese Scholar graciously accepted to brush in (hand write with a fine brush-like pen) information in Kanji, Hiragana and Katakana that you see in this book.

Usui Reiki Symbols

Your impressions and insights:

Usui Reiki Symbols

All what we call symbols are written statements and must be carefully written as they were originally intended to be.

One stroke can completely change the meaning of a word.

A Master symbol had been changed following the instruction of a psychic who explained the change will match the visiting Reiki practitioner's energy.

When reading the "new" written Master symbol, a Japanese laughed hard, saying he had not laughed like that for the last 16 years.

Myself, knowing what had been changed on the symbol: Instead of a man holding a torch, I wonder what in fact the man was holding.

Usui Reiki Symbols

Your impressions and insights:

Choku Rei
The Power symbol

Choku Rei

Workshop Hand-Out

This symbol is used in tantric Buddhism as well as in Shintoism. In tantric Buddhism there is an energy meditation that suggests to:

1. Visualize the energy entering your crown chakra.
2. From here let it flow into your first chakra.
3. Visualize the energy coming up to the seventh chakra.
4. From the seventh chakra the energy flows to the second chakra.
5. From the second chakra the energy flows to the fifth chakra.
6. From the fifth chakra the energy flows to the third chakra.
7. From the third chakra it flows to the fourth chakra.

Literally Choku Rei means « by imperial decree ». In shintoism this symbol is used as a command. You say what you would like to happen and then say three times « Choku Rei » in the sense of … so be it!

Nao Hi

<u>*Anny Slegten's notes*</u> *:*

By tradition, the Emperor is the re-incarnation of the Sun-God. When the Meiji Emperor was using the Choku Rei as we know it, it was carrying the message of « you do it or else ».

Choku Rei
The power symbol

Your impressions and insights:

Choku Rei

Nao Hi

Choku Rei
The power symbol

<u>Anny Slegten's notes</u> :

Choku Rei or Nao Hi in ancient Shintoism means « By decree of the Emperor » or « So be it ». When written in reverse it looses its meaning. Both Choku Rei or Nao Hi are used as a command.

To my understanding, the Choku Rei symbol we use is one of the oldest written affirmation. It comes from the country of BON, approximately 40,000 B.C., from a pre-Tibetan culture. It was explained to me that it is also where the Swastika comes from

The location is also approximately the location of present-day New Afghanistan. In Tibetan mythology, the country of BON was the ancient Holy Place ODDIYANA, where the 1st Buddha comes from.

Frank Arjava Petter mentioned a tantric Yoga meditation technique that uses the Choku Rei symbol. What is tantric? Here is from the Webster's New Collegiate Dictionary:

<u>Tantra/Tantric</u>:

<u>Sanskrit</u>: *Warp, from - he stretches, waves. Akin to Greek - to stretch. One of the later Hindu or Buddhism scriptures marked by mysticism and magic and used especially in the worship of Shakti.*

<u>Shakti</u>: *The dynamic energy of a Hindu god personified as his female consort.*

<u>Broadly</u>: *Cosmic energy as conceived in Hindu thought.*

Choku Rei

Nao Hi

Choku Rei

The power symbol

Your impressions and insights:

Choku Rei

Nao Hi

Tantric Yoga Meditation Technique
Let the energy radiate through the Heart Chakra.

Choku Rei
The power symbol

Choku Rei

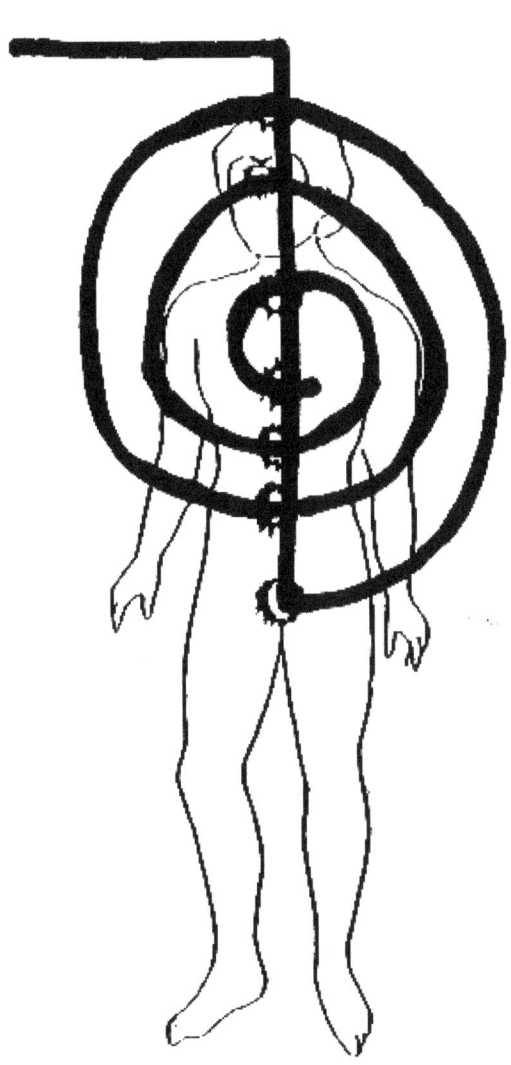

Nao Hi

Tantric Yoga Meditation Technique
Let the energy radiate through the Heart Chakra.

Choku Rei

The power symbol

<u>*Your impressions and insights:*</u>

Choku Rei

Nao Hi

Tantric Yoga Meditation Technique
Let the energy radiate through the Heart Chakra.

Choku Rei

The power symbol

<u>*Your impressions and insights:*</u>

Choku Rei

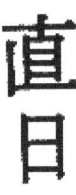

Nao Hi

Sei Heki

The mental healing symbol

性癖

Sei Heki

Workshop Hand-Out

This symbol is a derivative of the Sanskrit letter « Hrih ». Maybe because this is hard for the Japanese to pronounce, they name this symbol « Kiliku ». The last letter « u » in this word is hardly pronounced at all. In secret Japanese Buddhism, called Mikkyo this symbol represents the Amidah Buddha, the principle of love.

Anny Slegten's notes :

Chetna explained « Sei Heki » is written in two words and translates as inclination, a desire. When written in three words « Sei He Ki », it means happy and when we write « I Hei » it means a good fart! Since, then, I was informed the name is <u>Hring</u> – meaning God, instead of <u>Hrih,</u> and in Sanskrit, it is written as follows:

Indic   *Japanese*

Sei Heki

The mental healing symbol

<u>*Your impressions and insights:*</u>

Sei Heki

Sei Heki

The mental healing symbol

This symbol is of Sanskrit origin and changed with time. In Japan, the « symbols » are now written in Kanji. The Japanese Ladies who helped me with Kanji all explained Sei Heki means inclination with a sexual love meaning to it.

My conclusion is that the meaning and the purpose of this affirmation is the total self acceptance of self as a human being, and to be at peace with whom we are.

性癖

Sei Heki

Kiliku
As found in Mikkyo Temples

Although named differently, the Amidah Buddha can be found to purchase in many Buddhists stores by asking for the Buddha representing the principle of love.

I also noticed that the Buddha representing love has a Swastika on the Heart Chakra.

Sei Heki
The mental healing symbol

Your impressions and insights:

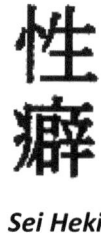

Sei Heki

Sei Heki

The mental healing symbol

<u>*Your impressions and insights:*</u>

性癖

Sei Heki

Hon Sha Ze Sho Nen
The distant healing symbol

Hon-Sha-Ze-Sho-Nen

Workshop Hand-Out

This symbol can be broken down into five individual Kanji, Chinese characters. It is used in esoteric Buddhism as well as in Shintoism. In Shintoism its meaning is « Man and god are one ».

A common practice in esoteric Buddhism is to add up several Kanji and then scramble them in order to get a certain energy.

Anny Slegten's notes :

When we started the course on symbols, the first thing Frank Arjava Petter did was to hold up an enlarged copy of the Hon Sha Ze Sho Nen and told us the good news: It is right!

Frank Arjava Petter was laboring on this symbol, wondering of its accuracy when a Buddhist Nun understood it immediately and proceeded to explain it. It is standard in esoteric Buddhism practice to take only a few strokes of each Kanji character and cramp them into one. To conclude the information on symbols, Frank explained the symbols are only a tool to focus. **The idea is to achieve a state of mind so one can focus without the symbols.**

Hon Sha Ze Sho Nen
The distant healing symbol

<u>*Your impressions and insights:*</u>

本者是正念

Hon-Sha-Ze-Sho-Nen

Hon Sha Ze Sho Nen
The distant healing symbol

HON
Book, source, origin.

SHA
Person.

ZE
Right, just.

SHO
Correct.

NEN
Thought, idea, wish.

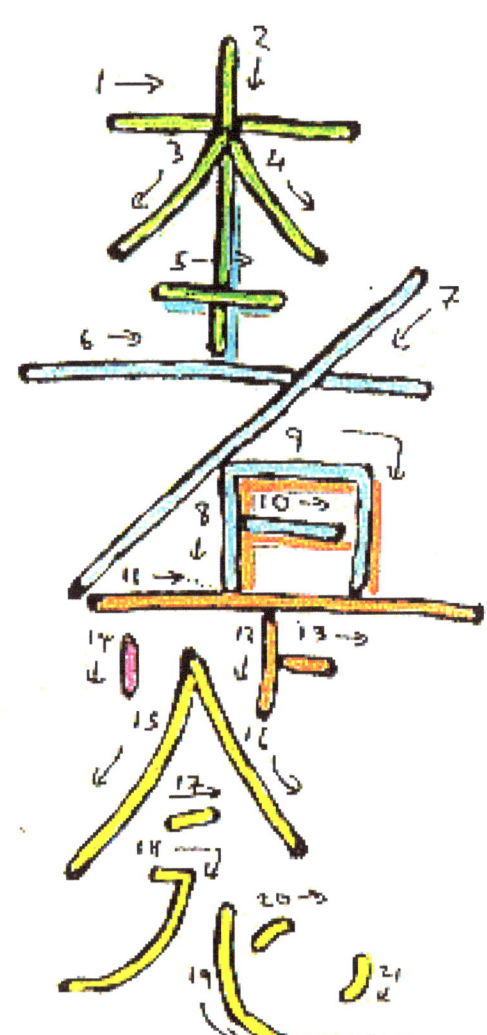

本者是正念

Hon-Sha-Ze-Sho-Nen

Hon Sha Ze Sho Nen
The distant healing symbol

<u>*Your impressions and insights:*</u>

本者是正念

Hon-Sha-Ze-Sho-Nen

Hon Sha Ze Sho Nen
The distant healing symbol

<u>*Your impressions and insights:*</u>

本者是正念

Hon-Sha-Ze-Sho-Nen

Mikao Usui, Reiki and the Japanese Culture

Mikao Usui

1865 - 1926

Old Kanji Brush

New Kanji Brush

Mikao Usui, Reiki and the Japanese Culture

Your impressions and insights:

Old Kanji Brush

New Kanji Brush

Mikao Usui, Reiki and the Japanese Culture

<u>*The following are Anny Slegten's personal notes:*</u>

A combination of:
- *what was known before the workshop,*
- *what was learned during the workshop,*
- *what was learned since.*

On Friday evening, the workshop started with an "ice breaker" led by Frank Arjava Petter and Chetna, his wife at the time. We were asked to get up to stretch, bending as far as we could forward, then backward, then to the left side, then to our right side, <u>moaning loudly</u>! This was done with much laughter.

Then Frank and Chetna started to explain some important facts of the Japanese culture: In Japan, Body, Mind and Spirit are ONE. It is considered as a unity.

The Japanese language has no logic; therefore translating a Japanese concept is not an easy task.

To make things more complicated to Westerners; there are three kinds of Japanese writing:

<u>Kanji</u>: *Chinese characters or ideographs each conveying an idea, most which have at least two readings. Kanji underwent a profound change during the World War II. As a result, the present generation cannot read Kanji as it was written prior to 1940.*

Old Kanji Brush

New Kanji Brush

Mikao Usui, Reiki and the Japanese Culture

Your impressions and insights:

Old Kanji Brush

New Kanji Brush

Mikao Usui, Reiki and the Japanese Culture

Hiragana: is a round writing and is taught since Kindergarten. It is a Japanese phonetic syllabary.

Katakana: A syllabary used primarily for foreign names and place names and words of foreign origin. The symbols are made up of straight lines.

Language is a living entity and changes with time. In present Japan, when written in Kanji, Reiki is understood as cult energy or ghost energy. Therefore, Reiki is now written in Katakana and Practitioners call it a relaxation technique or something similar.

Japanese people have a group identity. Doing everything together is a must. They must seem to be all the same. They stick together in the same company. "My group" is "The in group". Hence the Japanese saying: "The nail that sticks out must be hammered down". This was a survival technique. Starting in the 1400's with Portuguese, strangers would come to Japan, infiltrate groups, and kill. Even accepting someone they did not know in their own family circle could become a matter of life and death.

In Japan, Reiki is a totally closed society: The following is a list of Ryoho (healing method) Gakkai (association).

In 1999, Presidents of the Usui Reiki Ryoho Gakkai
Mikao Usui, Founder
Mr Ushida
Mr Taketomi
Mr Watanabe
Mr Wanami
Mrs Koyama

Usui Reiki
Ryoho Gakkai

Mikao Usui, Reiki and the Japanese Culture

Your impressions and insights:

Usui Reiki
Ryoho Gakkai

Mikao Usui, Reiki, and the Japanese Culture

They keep their membership to 500 (100 members in Tokyo), only replacing the ones that quit or die.

To learn Reiki, a member must attend a meeting once a week for at least 10 years. In 1999, the fee comes to the equivalent of U.S.$ 80.00 a month, and this, for 10 years or longer…

If for whatever reason a member cannot attend, the person often waits a long time before that particular lesson is given again. The group goes to Mikao Usui's shrine once a week, cleans it, and puts out flowers.

Frank Arjava Petter explained that Mikao Usui was a highly educated man. As a Secretary to the Foreign Minister, and later, Secretary to the Minister of Transport, Mikao Usui travelled in foreign countries – something unusual for a Japanese individual.

Mikao Usui discovered Reiki in March 1922 and incorporated his society in April of the same year. He died in 1926 at the age of 61.

Japanese are very cliquey. They fear a relationship with someone they don't know. They don't give information out, and they do not care of what is going out of their group and ultimately out of their country. They have the "Let these foreigners do their thing" attitude.

This way of thinking is easy to understand since, at that time, habitants in an area nautically close to Japan were raiding Japanese at night, stealing girls and women.

Old Kanji Print

New Kanji Print

Mikao Usui, Reiki and the Japanese Culture

<u>Your impressions and insights:</u>

Old Kanji Print

New Kanji Print

Mikao Usui, Reiki and the Japanese Culture

In addition, the political powers of the times wanted to eradicate Buddhism and Christianity. This meant letting someone they did not know into their circle could be a matter of life or death.

I have known since 1995 that a few manuscripts given by Mikao Usui to his students were still in existence. It is interesting to note the Usui Reiki Ryoho Gakkai accepted to give Frank Arjava Petter a copy of Mikao Usui's manuscript, only to give him a <u>computer printed</u> copy of Reiki Ryoho Hikkei (The most Important Methods for Reiki) written in old Kanji. Frank Arjava Petter had it translated and had it first published as "The Original Reiki Handbook of Dr. Mikao Usui".

When one considers all the teachings: At following our hands, at following our intuition, and the Usui Reiki Ryoho Gakkai's attitude of keeping the original information to themselves, I am not so sure this is Mikao Usui's handbook.

To me, it appears more as the handbook given out by Dr Hayashi, a Medical Doctor who created his own Medical Reiki Society. Not being a medical doctor, Mikao Usui was not a member of that Society.

In Japan, the Medical Doctor's office is called a Clinic. Dr Hayashi's Clinic had 8 beds, a large clinic by Japanese standards. He employed 16 Reiki Practitioners who worked around the clock.

Reiki Ryoho Hikkei

Mikao Usui, Reiki and the Japanese Culture

Your impressions and insights:

霊気療法必携

Reiki Ryoho Hikkei

Mikao Usui, Reiki and the Japanese Culture

From what I know, these practitioners were taking 3 months of their time at the clinic to pay off their Reiki tuition fee. Also, in Japan, Mikao Usui is referred to as Usui Sansei – teacher, or venerable teacher.

Mikao Usui was touching the body and hand healing was considered weird. Usui had difficulties with acceptance from his family. Instead of only sharing his discovery with his descendants and giving the presidency of the Usui Reiki Ryoho Gakkai to his son, he dared to make Reiki available to the public for the well being of humanity.

This is considered as disowning the family. After his death, Mikao Usui's name was never to be mentioned again in his family. Only his wife and his son are buried with him.

There were about 40 Reiki Schools in Japan before World War II.

Because of his work as secretary to several Ministers, Mikao Usui was well aware of the philosophies of the Meiji Emperor, and it is natural that he used some of the writings of the Meiji Emperor to convey his messages.

The Meiji Emperor was 15 years of age when he came to power. The Emperor was young and his advisers wanted him to eradicate Christianity and Buddhism. These were very bloody and brutal times. For years, I believed what we call the Reiki Precepts are actually Shintoism principles given by the Meiji Emperor to the public. It may be so.

Reiki Ryoho Hikkei

Mikao Usui, Reiki and the Japanese Culture

Your impressions and insights:

霊気療法必携

Reiki Ryoho Hikkei

Mikao Usui, Reiki and the Japanese Culture

In 2006, I had the privilege to attend a Reiki course given in Edmonton, Alberta, Canada by Reverent Hyakuten Inamoto. Coming from the spiritual lineage of Dr. Chujiro Hayashi and Chiyoto Yamaguchi, there were some differences in teachings compared to what we learned from Mrs. Hawayo Takata's spiritual lineage.

Everything being "orally reported" – it is not sure where the Reiki Precepts are coming from. All what is known is that Mikao Usui suggested meditating on the Five Precepts.

This information is in the image on the next page, which I received from Reverent Hyakuten Inamoto regarding the origins of the Reiki Precepts.

Mikao Usui, Reiki and the Japanese Culture

Your impressions and insights:

Mikao Usui, Reiki and the Japanese Culture

臼井霊気療法「教義」の原点（典拠）

大正3年（1914）12月28日発行の鈴木美山博士の著書「健全の原理」という書籍の巻頭に載っている「健全の道」という題の付いた以下の文言に基づき、臼井先生が創作されたと言われています。

「　今日だけは

　　　怒らず、恐れず、正直に、

　　　　　職務に励み、人に親切に　」　　美山

The Source of Usui Reiki Ryoho Principles (Five Precepts)

It is believed that Usui Sensei created so-called Five Principles or Five Precepts based on the phrase in the opening page of a book "Kenzen-no-genri" or "the Principle of Soundness" written by Dr. Suzuki Bizan, and published on December 28, in the 3rd year of Taisho (1914).

The PHRASE titled "A Path to Soundness" reads:
   [Today only
         Be not angry,
               Be not fearful,
                     With honesty,
                           Perform diligently your duty,
                                 Be kind to others.]
                                       By Bizan

KOMYO REIKI KAI
光明レイキ會

Do you remember that Kanji in Japanese means coming from China?

I have a framed picture of The Reiki Precepts written in Kanji before the Second World War.

My Chinese clients easily read the title we call The Reiki Precepts and explain, with pleasure, that it is:

"The Panacea for Good Luck".

Mikao Usui, Reiki and the Japanese Culture

Your impressions and insights:

Mikao Usui, Reiki and the Japanese Culture

Source: Webster's New Collegiate Dictionary

Buddhism:
A religion of eastern and central Asia growing out of the teaching of Gautama Buddha (563? - 483?BC originally Prince Siddhartha, Indian philosopher, founder of Buddhism) that suffering is inherent in life and that one can be liberated from it by mental and moral self-purification.

Christianity:
The religion derived from Jesus (4-8?BC-29? AD Jesus of Nazareth; the Son of Mary source of the Christian religion & Saviour in the Christian faith), based on the Bible as sacred scriptures, and professed by Eastern, Roman Catholic, and Protestant bodies.

Shintoism:
The indigenous religion of Japan consisting chiefly in the cultic devotion to deities of natural forces and veneration of the Emperor as a descendant of the sun-goddess.

In my search for the truth about Reiki, I came to realise that the only persons who have access to the manuals written by Mikao Usui and know the true methods used by Mikao Usui are the Presidents of the Usui Kyoho Gakkai. It is interesting to note they immediately reverted to the Japanese tradition of sharing it only with a few chosen ones.

Mikao Usui, Reiki and the Japanese Culture

Your impressions and insights:

Mikao Usui, Reiki and the Japanese Culture

I received information from many sources:

Visual accounts on Reiki classes of up to 40 students given in Tokyo by Toshitaka Mochizuki;

One of Toshitaka Mochizuki's books on Reiki that was translated to me, and an impressive amount of information and pictures that were enclosed with this book ordered from Japan;

I also received and read many accounts on Reiki classes given in small Japanese towns and in the country;

From conversations I had with Toshitaka Mochizuki, Frank Arjava Petter and his wife Chetna, and other Reiki Masters practising in Japan, I realised this:

The way Mikao Usui taught was the way things were taught in Japan in the 1920's. The "right" way to teach Reiki is by adapting the delivery of the information to the ability of the persons attending the class – to comprehend the system.

Reiki is not a technique. It is a realisation, an understanding at soul level, of the power that we were endowed as human beings. What is important is for the class to understand Usui Reiki demonstrates the power of our focus and our intent. "Symbols" and rituals are only tools to increase our focus. The power is within us.

Mikao Usui, Reiki and the Japanese Culture

Your impressions and insights:

Mikao Usui, Reiki and the Japanese Culture

Honoring Chetna Kobayashi's request

As I explained earlier in the book, we were asked to honour Chetna's request to not photocopy the Kanji. We were instructed to make our own, or find someone who will do it for us.

Back to Sherwood Park, Alberta, Canada, I was introduced to a Japanese Scholar fluent in the Japanese language who reads and writes the old and new Kanji, Hiragana and Katakana. These meetings were diverse learning experiences by themselves – on Japanese traditions and what we Westerners call "symbols".

After some explanations on my part, I obtained the permission to meet a Japanese Scholar who was agreeable to take the time to meet me.

Bringing with me the two books I had ordered from Japan, all written in Japanese and on the subject of Reiki, I realised what we call the back of a book is the front of the book in Japan, the book cover being at what we consider the back of the book.

Opening the book, all writing is done in vertical columns, from right to left, everything going from right to left.

From the little I knew, I had noticed that the majority is written in Kanji or in Katakana when considered a foreign word, and sometimes in Hiragana when appropriate.

Using a pointer, the Japanese Scholar was reading everything at great speed up and down each vertical column and from right to left, translating everything in English as she was following the pointer she was holding in her hand.

Mikao Usui, Reiki and the Japanese Culture

Your impressions and insights:

Mikao Usui, Reiki and the Japanese Culture

As the Japanese Scholar was reading one particular book, translating in English all along, she stopped and said Mikao Usui was a very wealthy man to have shared all his knowledge so willingly.

In Japan, a wealthy man shares his knowledge with anyone who is willing to learn – and pay for it. Poor people keep it within the family as this is considered an inheritance. This explains how come Mikao Usui's name was never to be mentioned in his family as they considered him having disowned his family.

I asked her to translate the impressive amount of advertising I had received along with the books. I was surprised... Even the number of attunements per affirmation (symbol) was explained – as well as the reason for it.

Photographs of each of the Reiki attunement positions were printed on a page, along with the reason for each Reiki attunement.

All this with pages and pages of testimonials – the majority hand written and all in vertical columns to be read from right to left.

In Japan, something you do not know is a secret to you. Therefore, observing someone, watching a film, or even reading something, does not give you an idea of what is involved in the procedure. Just like watching someone drive a car: It looks so easy until you are behind the wheel and discover there is much more to it than what meets the eye.

Mikao Usui, Reiki and the Japanese Culture

Your impressions and insights:

Mikao Usui, Reiki and the Japanese Culture

Frank Arjava Petter's second book "Reiki, The Legacy of Dr. Usui" was delivered to the hotel while giving the course I was attending in Detroit.

Talking about his first book, he explained he learned the hard way that intensive research is needed when receiving any information from anyone.

Trusting a Buddhist Nun, he believed her when she insisted he was making a mistake. From what she explained, Mikao Usui's correct name is Mikaomi Usui. Only when his first book "Reiki Fire" was printed, did he learn he had been mislead.

Asking the Japanese Scholar about it, she explained: In Japan, everyone is considered equal. One bows equally deep for the Emperor, or the school janitor.

Therefore, the only way to be better or superior, is to withhold some information to make sure the person asked is more informed than the asker.

I recommend these two books from Frank Arjava Petter: "Reiki Fire" and "Reiki, the Legacy of Dr. Usui". He lived in Japan for many years, and these books contain a wealth of valuable information about Reiki and the Japanese culture.

Mikao Usui, Reiki and the Japanese Culture

Your impressions and insights:

Mikao Usui, Reiki and the Japanese Culture

Your impressions and insights:

Mrs. Hawayo Takata

December 24, 1900 – December 11, 1980

Mrs. Hawayo Takata

Your impressions and insights:

Mrs. Hawayo Takata

Being the reason Reiki extended from Japan to the United States of America, the world, and then returned full circle to Japan – it is imperative I am writing about Mrs. Hawayo Takata.

Having learned the Japanese culture, I am admiring Mrs Hawayo Takata on her ability to incorporate her Japanese culture to the U.S.A. way of thinking.

Knowing that we do not know Kanji, she developed an interesting way to find out when a Reiki Master/Teacher was teaching Reiki and not paying her the established fee to do so.

Exotic cultures are fascinating subjects, and the Japanese culture is one of them – since we are mostly familiar with the Western cultures.

Understanding our fascination for what we perceived as the Japanese culture, Mrs. Hawayo Takata developed excellent marketing strategies. One of them was proclaiming that the Usui Reiki symbols are secrets. By Japanese standard, this is true. However, for us, a secret is something you hide and keep under cover.

Hence a way of teaching Reiki, Level 2 symbols was born. The ritual was the same each time I attended an Usui Reiki course, Level 2: Look at it, memorise it, and keep it secret.

Having usually written them on a plain peace of paper, the Reiki Master/Teacher would explain that since they are to be kept secret, she would burn them at the end of the day.

Mrs. Hawayo Takata

Your impressions and insights:

Mrs. Hawayo Takata

At first, I was not impressed with it all, until I learned and understood the Japanese way of thinking.

And now, laughing on how clever Mrs. Hawayo Takata was, I developed a sense a gratitude for her. She understood our curiosity about our perceived exotic side of Japan. Our beliefs of what was "secret" was one of many excellent marketing tools she used to make people want to learn Usui Reiki.

Now things have improved since we can check anything on the Internet. However, and to this day, the benefits of learning Reiki are constant. Usui Reiki in its simplicity is a solid foundation to understand the power residing within us – and how to use it.

Our thoughts are pure Energy.

Everything is Energy and Energy is everything.

With much Love and Light,

Anny Slegten

Mrs. Hawayo Takata

Your impressions and insights:

Mrs. Hawayo Takata

Your impressions and insights:

ONLINE STORE, CONTACT, AND MORE.

You may contact Anny by visiting any of her websites and scroll down the home page to the contact information.

http://www.annyslegten.com
      Anny's private website and online store.

http://www.success-and-more.com
      To find the description of the many services offered, and more.

http://www.htialberta.com
      The Hypnotism Training Institute of Alberta including descriptions of hypnosis and hypnotherapy courses given.

http://www.reiki-canada.com
      About the Reiki Training Centre of Canada.

http://www.slegtenianhypnosis.com
      Although open to anyone interested in this fascinating hypnosis modality, this website information is for graduates of the Hypnotism Training Institute of Alberta.

Other books by Anny Slegten

REIKI PURE AND SIMPLE

Volume I: The Sacred Rites

Anny J. Slegten

Reiki Training Centre of Canada
Class Material
http://www.reiki-canada.com

Other books by Anny Slegten

The Many Ways of Reiki
http://www.reiki-canada.com

Other books by Anny Slegten

The Reiki Training Centre of Canada
Teacher's Manual
http://www.reiki-canada.com

Other books by Anny Slegten

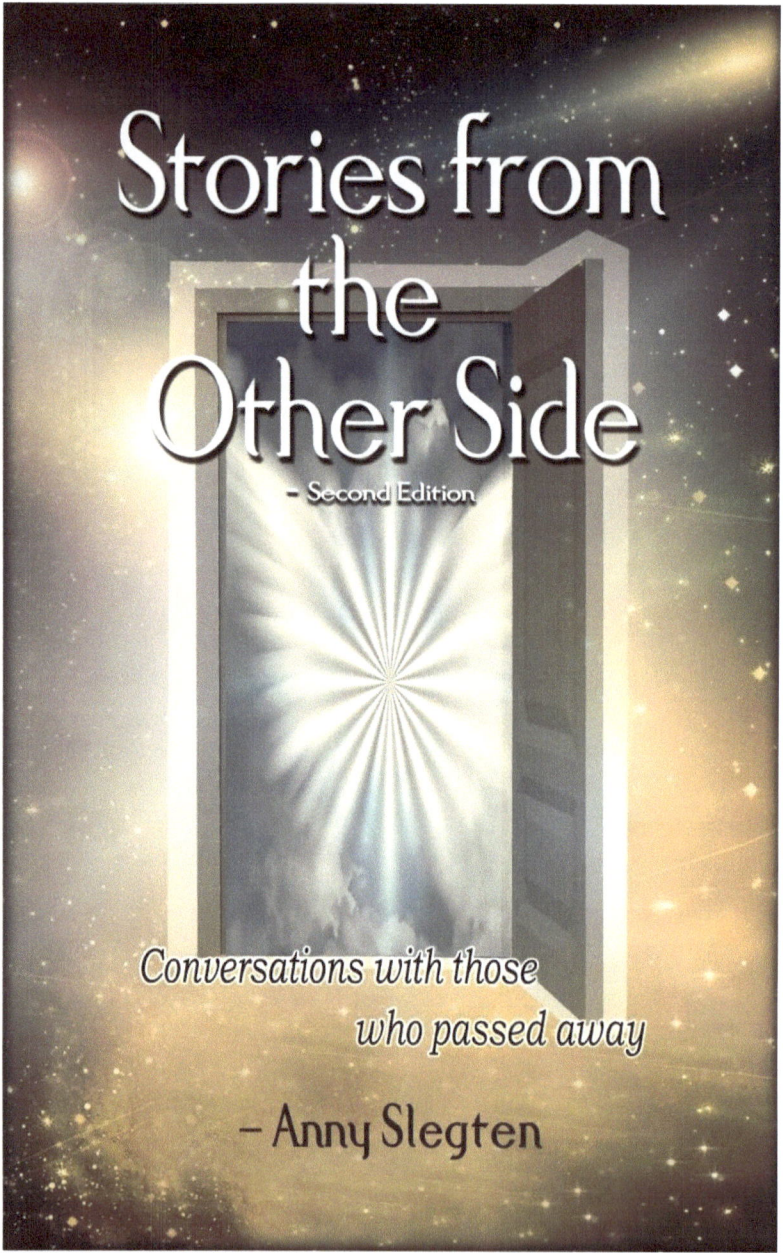

Stories From The Other Side – Second Edition
http://www.connectwithanny.com

Other books by Anny Slegten

The Four Mental Agreements
To Losing Weight
http://www.connectwithanny.com

Who is Anny Slegten?

A Reiki Master, Anny teaches the four levels of the "Usui Method of Natural Healing". This is known by the name of "Usui Reiki" as it presently is taught in Japan. It is also called "Traditional Japanese Reiki" as well as "Reiki" as practiced in North America.

Anny was formally introduced to Life Force Energy training in North Bay, Ontario, Canada, in 1976, and was initiated into Reiki in Alberta in March 1992.

Anny is grateful to all the Reiki Masters who helped her in her search for the source of the Usui System of Natural Healing known to us as Reiki.

Anny was initiated as a Reiki Master/Teacher in 1995. In 1996 she was initiated as a Tibetan Reiki Master/Teacher and took her Karuna™ Reiki Master/Teacher Training in February 1997.

In September 1999 Anny attended the Japanese Reiki Techniques Training maned "The Most Important Methods for Reiki" with Frank Arjava Petter – a Reiki Master/Teacher from Japan who is the author of many excellent books on Reiki.

In May 2006 Anny completed Komyo Reiki Shinpiden by Reverend Hyakuten Inamoto, who is an accredited Shihan/Teacher of the Koato Reiki Kai (Kyoto Center), Japan.

Anny's Belgian parents were from the Flemish part of Belgium and were speaking Flemish (Dutch) at home. Living in Congo, everything was in French.

Although she never spoke Flemish (Dutch), Anny speaks English with a guttural Dutch/German accent. Living in the English speaking part of Canada for decades, Anny now speaks French with an English accent!

As Director of The Hypnotism Training Institute of Alberta and The Reiki Training Centre of Canada, Anny has developed and structured the training and curriculum to the highest standards for both The Hypnotism Training Institute of Alberta and the Reiki Training Centre of Canada. She offers training to students that come from all over Canada and around the world.

Anny is an Author and holds certifications as:

- *Reiki Master/Teacher*
- *Master Remote Viewer*
- *Master Hypnotist*
- *Clinical Hypnotherapist*
- *Hypno-Baby Birthing Facilitator and Instructor*
- *HypnoBirthing Fertility Therapist for Men & Women*

Anny is a world renowned Clinical Hypnotherapist Hypnologist in full time practice since 1984 as well as an Hypno-Energy worker since 2008.

To know more about Anny, please visit http://www.annyslegten.com and make sure to look on her Blog.

Do you wonder what else Anny is publishing? Visit http://www.connectwithanny.com